ART as Science

Christine Fleming

children's press®

An imprint of Scholastic Inc.

NEW YORK • TORONTO • LONDON • AUCKLAND • SYDNEY
MEXICO CITY • NEW DELHI • HONG KONG
DANBURY, CONNECTICUT

© 2008 Weldon Owen Education Inc. All rights reserved.

No part of this publication may be reproduced or transmitted
in any form or by any means, electronic or mechanical,
including photocopying, recording, taping, or any information storage
and retrieval system, without permission in writing from the publisher.

Library of Congress Cataloging-in-Publication Data
Fleming, Christine, 1976-
  Art as science / by Christine Fleming.
      p. cm. -- (Shockwave)
  Includes index.
  ISBN-10: 0-531-17784-X (lib. bdg.)
  ISBN-13: 978-0-531-17784-6 (lib. bdg.)
  ISBN-10: 0-531-15461-0 (pbk.)
  ISBN-13: 978-0-531-15461-8 (pbk.)
  1. Art and science--Juvenile literature. I. Title. II. Series.

  N72.S3F54 2007
  701'.05--dc22
  2007008937
  2007007238

Published in 2008 by Children's Press, an imprint of Scholastic Inc.,
557 Broadway, New York, New York 10012
www.scholastic.com

SCHOLASTIC, CHILDREN'S PRESS, and associated logos are trademarks
and/or registered trademarks of Scholastic Inc.

08 09 10 11 12 13 14 15 16 17
10 9 8 7 6 5 4 3 2 1

Printed in China through Colorcraft Ltd., Hong Kong

Author: Christine Fleming
Editor: Mary Atkinson
Designer: Carol Hsu
Photo Researchers: Jamshed Mistry and Sarah Matthewson

Every effort has been made to trace and acknowledge copyright. Where this attempt has proved
unsuccessful, the publisher would be pleased to hear from the photographer or party concerned
to rectify any omissions.

Photographs by: AGE, W.Bibikow/www.stockcentral.co.nz (pp. 6–7); **Anne Luo** (p. 1; p. 5; fractal,
pp. 22–23; op-art circles, p. 25); **Jennifer and Brian Lupton** (p. 30; girl pointing, p. 31); **Getty
Images** (dancers, sculptor, p. 9; weaver, p. 13; cave art, pp. 14–15; Egyptian stone cat, p. 20;
Han van Meegeren trial, p. 21; science photographer, p. 29); **© 2007 The M. C. Escher Company-
Holland. All rights reserved. www.mcescher.com** (M. C. Escher's *Convex and Concave*, 1955
Lithograph, cover; M. C. Escher's symmetry drawing E103, pp. 22–23; M. C. Escher's *Waterfall*,
1961, pp. 24–25); **National Geographic Image Collection** (skull holograms, p. 27); **Photolibrary**
(Leon Battista Alberti, p. 8; Sphinx, p. 14; X-ray of Titian painting, p. 18; infrared scanner, p. 19;
forgery, p. 21; music score, p. 28); **Stock.Xchng** (clogs, p. 13; pyramid, pp. 10–11); **Tranz/Corbis**
(church, p. 8; columns, p. 10; Rupmati Pavilion, Hypobank, p. 11; p. 12; Sistine Chapel restoration,
p. 15; *Bacchus and Ariadne*, pigment pot, p. 17; conservator at work, pp. 18–19; mandala, p. 23;
Vega-Nor, p. 24; still from *Final Fantasy*, pp. 26–27; Jacqueline Kennedy Onassis, p. 27;
making digital music, pp. 28–29; photographer, p. 29; girl with microscope, pp. 30–31)

All other illustrations and photographs © Weldon Owen Education Inc.

CONTENTS

Samoan pattern on bark cloth

architect (*AR kuh tekt*) a person who designs buildings

canvas a piece of fabric on which an artist paints

commission to hire someone to do a particular piece of work

fractal an image created using a math formula. A fractal consists of a pattern that repeats itself on smaller and smaller scales.

perspective the art of drawing or painting a scene so that forms and objects appear to have the same shapes and relative sizes as they do in real life. For example, distant objects are smaller than nearer ones.

pigment a richly colored substance that is used to impart color to other materials

sculpture a piece of art carved or shaped out of a material such as stone, wood, clay, or metal

tessellation a pattern created out of geometric shapes that fit together without any gaps

. . . .

For easy reference, see Wordmark on back flap.

For additional vocabulary, see Glossary on page 32.

The word *tessellation* comes from *tessera*, the Greek root for *four*. A tessera is a small, often square, tile used in a mosaic. When many tesserae are put together, they become a tessellation.

Today, most people think of art and science as separate subjects. But they are related. Some of the greatest minds have combined creative and scientific ideas. In the 1400s, Leonardo da Vinci studied the human body to make his paintings more realistic. He went on to produce outstanding artworks. He also made some important scientific discoveries.

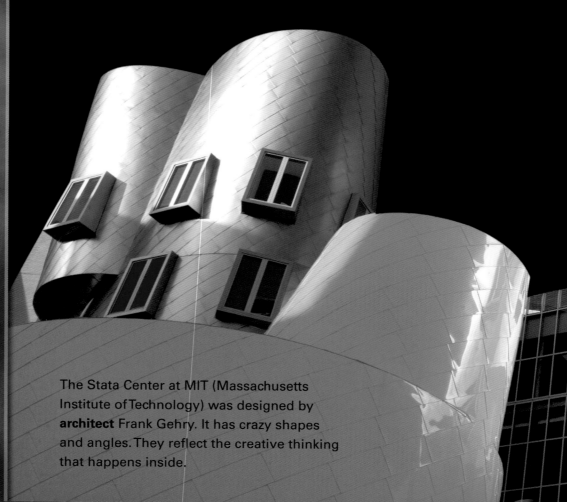

The Stata Center at MIT (Massachusetts Institute of Technology) was designed by **architect** Frank Gehry. It has crazy shapes and angles. They reflect the creative thinking that happens inside.

Thinking to do with science and math takes place mainly in our brain's left side. Thinking to do with art and other creative subjects takes place mainly in our brain's right side. There are many ways that we can use both halves of our brains to produce exciting results. Many creative people, such as architects, have jobs with science or math content. Some people, such as art **restorers**, even use science to save works of art!

MASTER THE ART

When we talk about the arts, we usually mean such things as painting, **sculpture**, and music. But this was not always the case. In the past, the arts included any skill that someone had mastered. People who studied art in **Renaissance** times learned languages, math, and music. They also learned science, painting, sculpture, and architecture.

Leon Battista Alberti lived in Renaissance Italy. He excelled in math, architecture, painting, poetry, and sports. He was what we now call a Renaissance man.

This church in Italy was designed by Alberti in 1470.

Santa Maria Novella, Florence, Italy

We need special talent to do well in some arts. We call these the fine arts. Painting, drama, and literature are fine arts. The purpose of a fine art is mainly to give pleasure. It is also to pass on ideas. Other arts are called useful arts. These include cooking and weaving. They have an everyday purpose. However, they also allow people to express their creativity.

Some artists earn their living from their work. For many others, art is a hobby. They enjoy being creative. However, they may not wish to make art their profession.

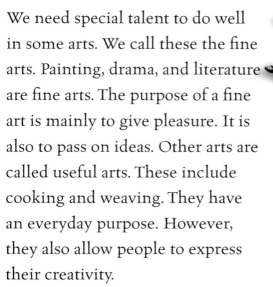

We often call dance an art rather than a sport. This is because it is more to do with creativity [aesthetics] than competition [athletics].

We use the term *master the art* for just about any skill. We say, "She has mastered the art of playing the guitar." Here we are using the word *art* to mean a highly developed skill.

Sculpture is a fine art. It allows artists to express their **traditions** and their own ideas.

9

SHAPING UP

Throughout history, powerful rulers have hired talented architects. The architects have designed palaces, tombs, and public buildings. They have used science and math to ensure their buildings are strong and practical. They have used their artistic skills to design enduring **masterpieces**.

Many of the shapes chosen by architects have a practical purpose. Rows of columns allow walls to be lightweight. Curved arches can support greater weights than straight beams. Domed roofs are stronger than flat roofs.

This Mayan pyramid was built around 1200 A.D. It has 365 steps.

Pyramid of Kukulkan, Mexico

I already know that the Mayans were interested in calendars. I also know that there are 365 days in most years. So maybe the 365 steps on the pyramid represent the passing of a year.

Pyramids are strong, stable structures. In ancient times, architects chose pyramids as tombs for their greatest rulers. They knew that a huge stone pyramid would last thousands of years.

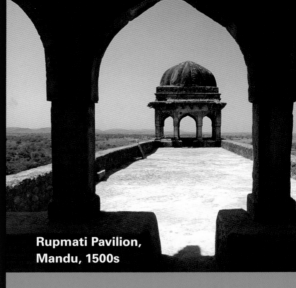

Rupmati Pavilion, Mandu, 1500s

Many Indian palaces have arches, domes, and columns.

SHOCKER

In the 1200s, architects in Europe competed to build the highest **cathedral**. The contest ended in 1284. That was when Beauvais Cathedral in France collapsed. It had been about 173 feet high.

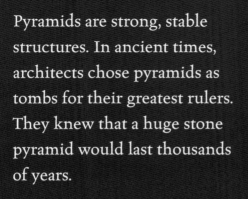

Hypobank building, Munich, Germany

This building has distinctive columns. They look as if they are held onto the building with giant clamps.

EVERYDAY ART

Austrian house

The homes of ordinary people are also combinations of technology and art. In many places, a traditional style has developed over centuries. For example, an Austrian house always has a sloped roof. This allows heavy snow to slide off. Its wooden carvings and flower boxes add beauty and color. The mud-walled homes of the Ndebele people of South Africa keep out the hot sun. The Ndebele women often decorate the walls with colorful patterns.

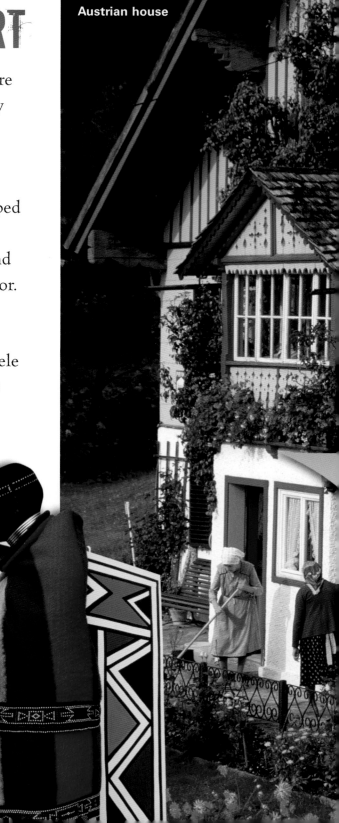

Ndebele woman painting her home

Today, many people make traditional crafts for pleasure or to sell. In the past, people created these things to use them. Stores did not sell many ready-made goods. Instead, most women made their own clothes and household items. Men often made their own tools and furniture. There were no TVs or computers for entertainment. Instead, people often spent time decorating the things they made. Many people took pride in crafting useful, attractive items.

Weaving is a traditional craft. Fibers such as straw, wool, or flax are used. They are woven into many things, including hats and rugs.

Wooden clogs are practical footwear for farmers or people who work outdoors. In Holland, some workers still wear them. Clogs keep their feet clean, dry, and safe. Today, they are often painted in bright colors and sold as souvenirs.

Ancient Art, Modern Science

Ancient art teaches us about the past. From cave art, scientists figure out what mattered to people thousands of years ago. Historians study **medieval** paintings. They use them to see how people used to dress and live.

Experts work to repair and protect old art. If they didn't do so, it would be lost forever. The science of repairing art is called art restoration. Art **conservation**, on the other hand, protects art from future damage. Some restorers and conservators work on huge ancient monuments. Others work on small paintings. There is great skill involved in restoration and conservation. Workers must protect the art. They must also keep it as close to its original form as possible.

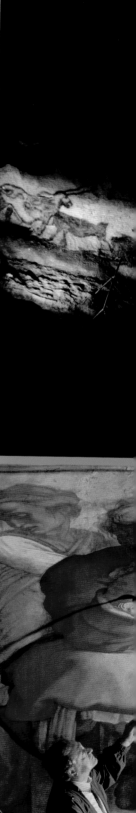

The Great Sphinx was covered in scaffolding for much of the 1990s. About 100,000 stones were used to repair it.

In 1940, four French teenagers discovered some cave art at Lascaux, in southern France. The art was 17,000 years old. There are about 600 painted animals and 1,500 engravings on the cavern walls. However, a spreading fungus recently threatened to destroy the art. Scientists are working to save it.

SHOCKER

In the past, many restorers did more harm than good. Today, restorers often spend much of their time fixing the work of restorers from 100 years ago.

In 1508, artist Michelangelo began painting the ceiling of Rome's Sistine Chapel. Nearly 500 years later, restorers used computers to repair his work.

Pigment and Paint

In medieval times, most people couldn't read. Religious leaders **commissioned** artworks to remind people of Bible stories. There was no photography, so rich people commissioned portraits of themselves. They wanted to be remembered after they had died.

People wanted artworks to last. It was important that the paint not fade or flake off. Until recently, artists made their own paints. Colorful plants, soils, and stones were used to make **pigments**. Some pigments were rare and expensive. For example, blue pigment was made by grinding lapis lazuli. This is a semi-precious stone. The pigment was mixed with a binder to make paint. In the **Middle Ages**, many artists painted with tempera. This had an egg-yolk binder. In the fifteenth century, oil became the binder of choice.

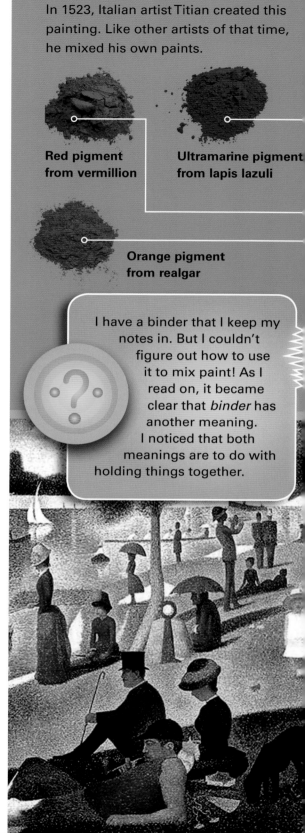

In 1523, Italian artist Titian created this painting. Like other artists of that time, he mixed his own paints.

Red pigment from vermillion

Ultramarine pigment from lapis lazuli

Orange pigment from realgar

I have a binder that I keep my notes in. But I couldn't figure out how to use it to mix paint! As I read on, it became clear that *binder* has another meaning. I noticed that both meanings are to do with holding things together.

Bacchus and Ariadne

These colorful pigments were found in an ancient Egyptian architect's tomb. They were placed there about 3,400 years ago.

Traditionally, artists mix their colors before painting. In the late 1800s, artist Georges Seurat created color in a new way. He put thousands of tiny colored dots on his **canvas**. From a distance, the eye blends the colors. This creates the shades Seurat wanted the viewer to see.

Sunday Afternoon on the Island of La Grande Jatte, **1886**

Seurat's style is called pointillism. From close up, the viewer can see the tiny colored dots.

17

The Tools of the Trade

Conservators and restorers need to fix and clean artworks without harming them. To do this, they often use special tools. They use microscopes to get a close look. They also use techniques involving **infrared rays**, **X-rays**, and **lasers**.

In X-radiography, art experts produce images the same way as doctors make X-rays of bones. X-rays are fired at a painting. Depending on the thickness of the paint and the kinds of paint used, more or fewer X-rays pass through the painting. Those that get through strike photographic paper on the other side. This creates an image. The image provides information about all the paint layers in a painting.

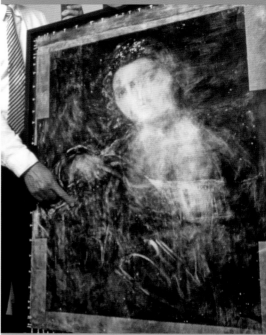

This X-ray image shows how the artist Titian changed the position of a woman's head. Both heads show in the X-ray image.

Infrared rays reach deeper into a painting than ordinary light rays. In one technique, infrared light is used to see if there are pencil or charcoal marks under the paint. The infrared light is shone onto the painting. Special cameras pick up the infrared light that reflects off the painting. Any black marks under the paint appear black on screen. This is because the chemicals in the pencil or charcoal do not reflect the infrared light.

An infrared scanner moves across a painting. The whole painting is scanned. Then the machine produces a black-and-white image. It reveals any sketches beneath the paint.

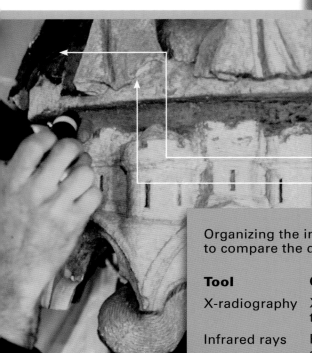

Conservators often use lasers to clean sculptures and carved stone. The lasers produce powerful pulses of infrared light. This heats the dirt. It makes it expand and flake off.

○ **Uncleaned stone**

○ **Cleaned stone**

Organizing the information helps me to compare the different techniques.

Tool	Characteristic	Purpose
X-radiography	X-rays pass through painting	To gather info about paint layers
Infrared rays	Rays reflect off some surfaces	To see pencil lines under the paint
Lasers	Produce pulses that heat dirt	To clean sculptures and carved stone

FAKE!

Artworks by famous artists sell for millions of dollars. So do very old artworks. As a result, many people have tried to create fake artworks. Often it is very hard to tell what is real and what is not. Experts use many techniques to uncover the fakes. One useful technique is called X-ray diffraction. Tiny samples of paint are analyzed using X-rays. This technique reveals a sample's exact chemical content.

Portrait of a Woman (below right) was once thought to have been painted by the Spanish artist Francisco Goya. X-ray diffraction of a speck of white paint showed that it was zinc white. This paint was invented after Goya died. An X-radiograph of the painting showed another painting underneath. The cracks in the original painting had been used to make the fake painting look old.

This ancient Egyptian sculpture is now thought to be a fake.

There are many English words with similar meanings to the word *fake*. Some of them are: *forgery, fraud, counterfeit, bogus, false, phony*.

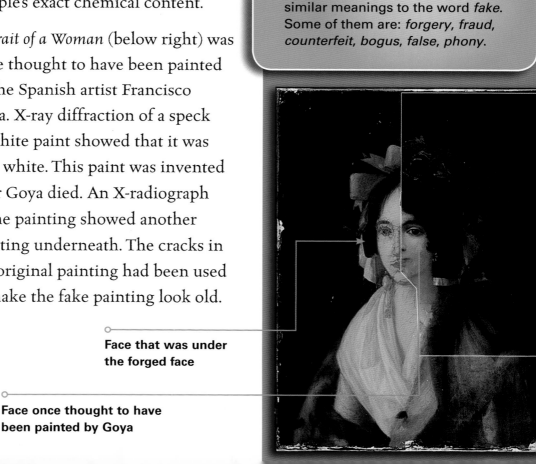

Face that was under the forged face

Face once thought to have been painted by Goya

Some of the techniques used to study masterpieces are also used to detect forgeries. For example, many paintings are examined under **ultraviolet (UV) light**. The UV light makes some paints **fluoresce**. The amount of fluorescence depends on the pigments and their age. This helps the experts figure out which pigments were used.

This forgery was examined under UV light. Dark blotches showed up. They revealed where the paint had been retouched.

THE MASTER FORGER

Han van Meegeren was a famous Dutch forger. During World War II, he created six paintings. They were supposedly by the seventeenth-century Dutch painter Johannes Vermeer. He sold the paintings to German officers for huge sums of money. The fakes were hard to detect. Van Meegeren had used mainly pigments available when Vermeer was alive in the 1600s. He also used old canvases. However, chemical analysis showed that the paints contained a modern plastic binder. It had not been invented in Vermeer's time.

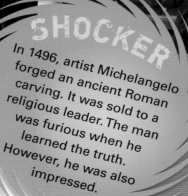

This is van Meegeren at his trial in 1947. One of his forged paintings is hanging behind him.

SHOCKER

In 1496, artist Michelangelo forged an ancient Roman carving. It was sold to a religious leader. The man was furious when he learned the truth. However, he was also impressed.

ART AND MATH

The branch of math that involves studying shapes is called geometry. It involves 2-D shapes. These include squares, triangles, and circles. It also involves 3-D forms. These include cubes, pyramids, and spheres. When these shapes are combined in repetitive ways, they create patterns. The artist M. C. Escher created fascinating images by linking 2-D shapes in patterns with no gaps. These patterns are called **tessellations**.

Another kind of artwork created using the rules of math is a **fractal**. Each fractal is actually a graph of a math equation. Computers are needed to create complex fractal images.

Geometry	
2-D Shapes	**3-D Forms**
square	cube
triangle	pyramid
circle	sphere

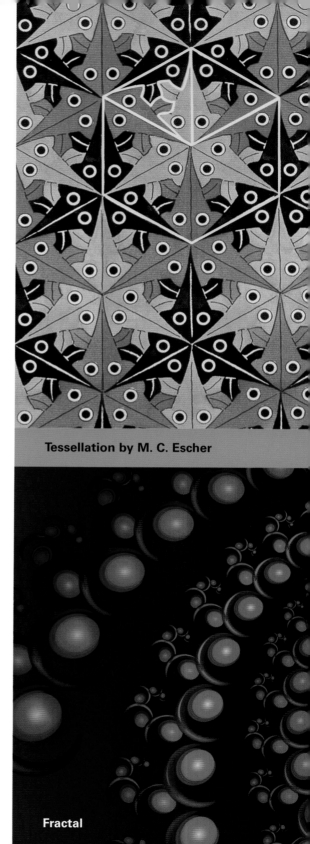

Tessellation by M. C. Escher

Fractal

Tapa cloth is made by some Pacific Island cultures. It is decorated with geometric patterns.

Some traditional Buddhist artworks show circles and other geometric shapes. They are symbols of the universe and are called mandalas.

THE ART OF ILLUSION

To paint a realistic scene, an artist must master the art of **perspective**. Some artists have twisted the rules of perspective. They create illusions that fool the mind. This kind of art is called optical art, or op art. Some op-art images seem to make sense until you look closely. Some appear to be 3-D. Others look as if they are moving. Artists create these images using repetition of simple forms. The forms often include circles and **parallel** lines.

Vega-Nor by Victor Vasarely, 1969

Waterfall by M. C. Escher, 1961. Does the water flow along a flat surface or upward?

PERSPECTIVE

Artists often imagine lines coming out of an object to meet at one or more points in the distance. This helps them achieve realistic angles.

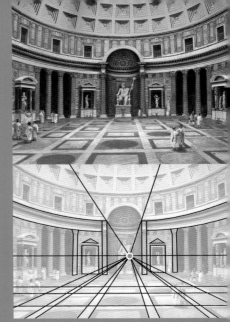

One-point perspective

One-point perspective

Two-point perspective

Is this image really moving, or does it just appear to move?

25

TECHNOLOGY AND ART

As technology has advanced, so has art. No sooner had photography and film been invented than artists began to use these new mediums. Movie makers and computer-game creators constantly push technology to its limits. Today, special effects are often created using computers. Techno-wizards transform ordinary movie scenes into magical fantasy worlds. They work to make their animated characters more and more realistic. Production companies compete to make each new movie more spectacular than the last.

Techno-wizard is a new word. It is used to describe people who are clever at using technology. Some related words are: *techno-fear*, *techno-mall*, *techno-geek*, *techno-stress*.

The movie *Final Fantasy: The Spirits Within* was released in 2001. The characters were not acted by real people. They were CGIs – computer-generated images.

MAKING A HOLOGRAM

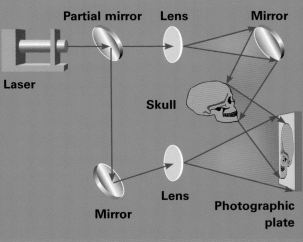

Laser
Partial mirror
Lens
Mirror
Skull
Mirror
Lens
Photographic plate

Much twentieth-century art was experimental. New techniques were mixed with old ones. In this 1963 portrait of Jacqueline Kennedy, artist Andy Warhol enlarged a photo. He then altered it using colored inks.

A hologram is a 3-D image. It is made using laser light. The laser beam is split into two beams. One beam shines on a photographic plate. The other beam bounces off the object and then onto the plate. Where the two beams meet, a pattern forms on the plate. When the plate is developed, a 3-D image appears. It seems to hover in front of the plate.

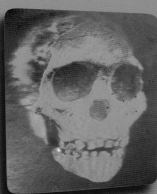

Front view   **Side view**

This holographic skull featured on the November 1985 cover of *National Geographic* magazine. The viewer sees slightly different views of the skull when looking from different angles.

MUSIC AND MUCH MORE

Music is another field that combines art and science. Many instruments have notes that go up in steps. Scientists know that each note makes the air **vibrate** at a particular rate per second. Today, machines can create these tones electronically. Musicians use computers to compose music. They also use machines called synthesizers. They can create almost any sound they can imagine. However, just like all musicians, they still need talent to create good music.

A piece of music can be translated into a form of writing. For hundreds of years, people have used musical notation to write down their **compositions**.

Architecture, film, and music are just some of the fields where art and science support each other. Take a look at the world around you. How are the things you can see influenced by the worlds of art and science? The page you are looking at right now is just one example.

Science photographer

DID YOU KNOW?

People have been writing music for thousands of years. The first-known written music is about 4,500 years old. It came from the Middle East.

Here are some careers that combine art and science:

- Science photographer
- Computer animator
- Art restorer
- Computer-game creator
- Architect
- Fashion designer
- Graphic artist

Computer animator

Talented DJs can mix music and sounds digitally at a club, while people are dancing.

Some people think that they can't be good at both **logic**-based subjects and creative subjects. However, geniuses such as Leonardo da Vinci show us that this is not true. In fact, many ordinary people have careers that combine art and science.

WHAT DO YOU THINK?

Should high-school students be allowed to specialize in just the arts or the sciences?

PRO

There is too much information available these days for everyone to know about everything. We need to specialize. Also, students will enjoy school and stay longer if they can do the things they enjoy.

At many high schools, students choose their subjects. Some do mainly science. Others do mainly arts. This helps them prepare for some college courses. But it also means they stop learning in one area or the other.

CON

I think people limit themselves and their futures too soon. We should all have a broad education. That way, we will be able to combine scientific and artistic ideas as adults. It will keep our brains active and make us more interesting people.

Go to **www.tessellations.org** to learn more about art and science.

31

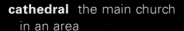

GLOSSARY

cathedral the main church in an area

composition a complex piece of music

conservation the process of protecting artworks and other valuable objects from damage

fluoresce (*FLUH ress*) to give off light, or to glow, when energy is absorbed

infrared ray an energy ray with a slightly longer wavelength than visible light. We feel some infrared rays as heat.

laser a machine that produces a narrow, powerful beam of light of a particular wavelength

logic thinking that involves reasoning and following steps to reach correct answers

masterpiece an outstanding work of art or craft

medieval to do with the Middle Ages

Middle Ages the period in European history from about 500 A.D. to about 1500 A.D.

parallel two lines that are always exactly the same distance apart and never meet or cross

Renaissance (*REN uh sahnts*) a period in European history that lasted from the 1300s until about 1600. The Renaissance (meaning "rebirth") was marked by advances in art, literature, and science.

restorer a person who fixes damaged artworks or other valuable objects

tradition something, such as a belief or a craft, that is handed down through generations

ultraviolet light energy rays with a shorter wavelength than visible light. Ultraviolet, or UV, rays make some materials fluoresce.

vibrate to move back and forth at a very fast pace

X-ray an energy ray with a much shorter wavelength than visible light. X-rays can pass through some solid objects but not others.

INDEX